Modeling Clay

with 3 basic shapes

B.E.S.
PUBLISHING

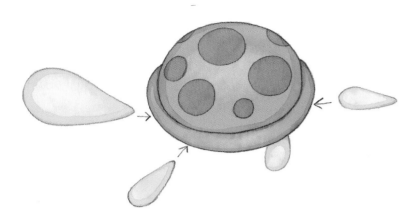

Contents

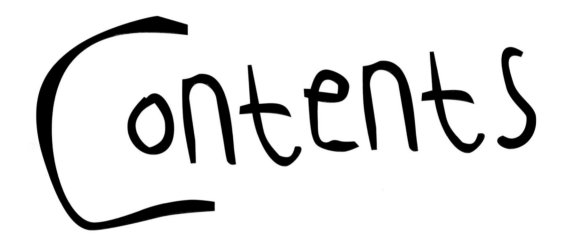

- Techniques 4
- I'm a **rhino** 8
- My name is Derek the **Duck** 10
- I'm a **snail** 12
- My name is Grumpy **Dino** 14
- I'm a **bear** 16
- My name is Pearl the **Penguin** 18
- I'm a **puppy** 20
- My name is Mary the **Mouse** 22
- I'm an **owl** 24
- My name is Bradley the **Bunny** 26
- I'm a **bee** 28
- I'm a **crocodile** 30
- My name is Eric the **Elephant** 32
- I'm a **chicken** 34
- My name is Skip the **Seal** 36
- I'm a **frog** 38
- My name is Fiona the **Fox** 40
- I'm a **worm** in an apple 42
- My name is Sam the **Salamander** 43
- My name is Holly the **Hedgehog** 44
- I'm a **hippo** 46
- My name is Kelly the **Koala** 48
- I'm a **turtle** 50

- My name is Fran the **Fish** 52
- I'm a **cow** 54
- My name is Sid the **Snake** 56
- I'm an **octopus** 57
- I'm a **kitten** 58
- My name is Betty the **Bird** 60
- I'm a **chick** 62
- My name is Simon the **Squirrel** 64
- I'm a **ladybug** 66
- My name is Ray the **Reindeer** 68
- I'm a **toucan** 70
- My name is Penelope the **Pony** 72
- I'm a **panda** 74
- My name is Shelly the **Sheep** 76
- I'm a **hamster** 78
- My name is Brenda the **Butterfly** 80
- I'm a **monkey** 82
- My name is Leo the **Lion** 84
- I'm a **raccoon** 86
- My name is Daphne the **Deer** 88
- I'm a **wolf** 90
- I'm a **kangaroo** 92
- My name is Willy the **Whale** 94

MATERIALS

You don't need special tools for working with modeling clay. You may have everything you need around the house, like straws, a rolling pin or pencil, toothpicks, paintbrushes, lids, markers, marbles, poster board, thick nylon wires, and twigs.

Techniques

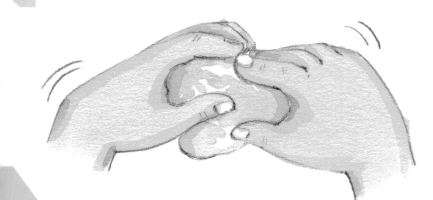

MAKING NEW COLORS

You can buy modeling clay in the colors you want or you can create your own. You just have to mix two or more colors together well, in the amounts you decide. Knead them together until you have an even color. Play around and invent new colors. It's so much fun!

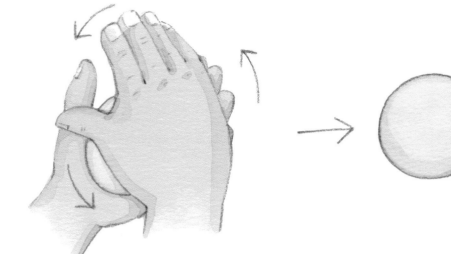

HOW TO MAKE A BALL

Take some clay and rub it between the palms of your hands, while rolling it around and pressing. You'll have a round shape in no time at all! If you need to, you can smooth it over with your finger.

HOW TO MAKE A TEARDROP

First make a ball, like above. Then, put it on the table and press down on one side with your fingers flat, moving them slowly up and down. This will make a teardrop shape. You can make it smoother with your finger. If you cut the thick part of the teardrop, you'll get a cone, which can also be a triangle if you flatten it.

HOW TO MAKE A WORM

Once again, you will start with a ball. Then, roll it on a table with your fingers flat and pressed together, or between the palms of your hands. Keep rolling it until you have a worm the thickness you need.

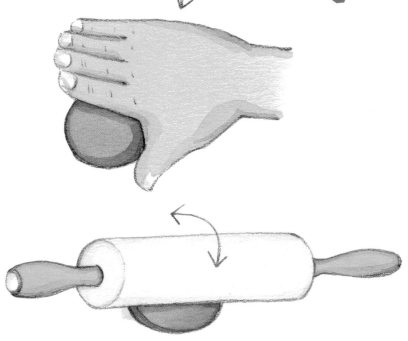

FLAT SHAPES

Use the palm of your hand to squash a shape onto the table. If the shape is small, you can flatten it with your finger. And, if you want to make it really thin and even, you could use a rolling pin. Remember to put paper down first so the clay doesn't stick to the table.

DOTS & STRIPES

If you flatten little balls of one color onto a different-colored shape, you'll get dots. If you flatten worms, they turn into stripes.

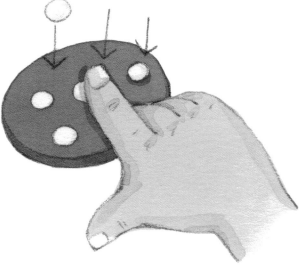

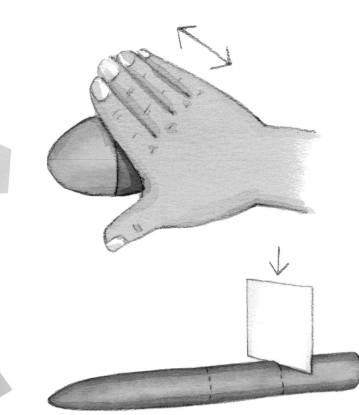

JOINING TWO COLORS

After joining two pieces of different colors, smooth them together with your fingers or by rolling it (if you can) with your fingers flat and pressed together.

CUTTING

To cut pieces of clay, you can use a piece of poster board.

STRENGTHENING

When joining two pieces so they stay together well, strengthen the joint from behind by smoothing it with your finger. This makes the clay move from one side to the other and, you'll notice your figure getting stronger.

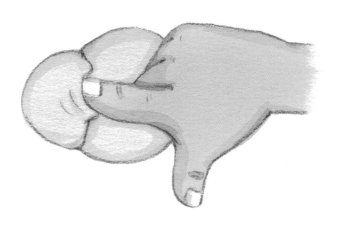

MARKS, DENTS, & LINES

Poster board is very useful for making marks in the clay, both straight and curved, like mouths and eyelids. You can also use toothpicks to draw on shapes and lines.

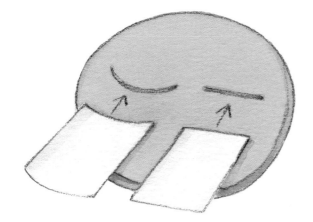

HOLES

Depending on how big of a hole you need to make, you can use different tools. You can use a toothpick for tiny holes, the sharp end of a pencil for holes of different sizes (depending on how far you insert it), the handle of a paintbrush for medium-sized holes, and a marker or marble for large round holes.

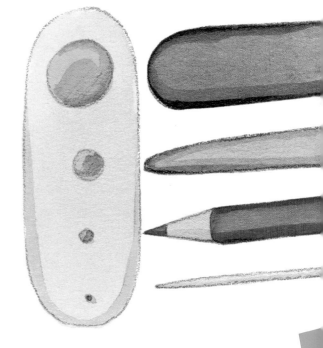

FACES & TEXTURES

Straws work really well for making small mouths and closed eyes. They also work great for making textures like fish scales and feathers. You can stick them into the clay straight or at an angle. Experiment to find what you like!

I'm a rhinO

1. Shape a piece of clay into a ball for the rhino's body. Then, make a smaller ball in a lighter color. Cut it in half and stick it onto the large ball.

1

2. Use four little balls for his legs. Press them on so that the body is stable.

2

3. Make two holes in the snout with a pencil, and then stick on two tiny black balls for the eyes.

3

4

4. Use a piece of poster board to carve the shape of his mouth. Mold the ears into two teardrop-shaped pieces.

5. Roll a small piece of clay between your hands to make a thin tail. And, finally and most importantly…the rino's horn! Make a small triangular shape with white clay and stick it on his nose.

5

I love my horn!

9

1. Use a ball for the head and a larger teardrop shape for the duck's body. Stick the two pieces together and you have your duck!

2. Roll out a log in another color, flatten it, and cut off one end. Stick it to his head to make the beak.

3. To make the eyes, roll two little white balls, flatten them, and stick them to his head.

My name is Derek the Duck

4. To make his pupils, just flatten two little black balls and stick them onto the eyes.

5. To finish, make two small teardrop shapes and flatten them slightly for the wings. Stick one onto each side of Derek's body.

Does anyone want to play with me?

I'm a Snail

1. Use two different colors and roll them into long thin teardrop shapes. One will be the snail's body. Raise up the thick part of your teardrop like in the picture. Now, make the shell with the other piece.

2. Roll this piece up into a spiral, starting with the thinner end. Then, cut off the thick end.

3. Now, press the two pieces together.

4. You'll need three different balls to make each eye: one the same color as the body, one white, and another tiny black one. Use two toothpicks and stick them into the head to create the eyes, as shown.

5. Finally, make the nose with a little ball of clay that's the same color as the body.

It's raining a lot. Yay!

My name is GRUmpy Dino

1. Make a round ball for the dino's body. Mold a teardrop shape for the tail, and then cut it diagonally at the thick end. Join the two pieces and smooth them using your finger.

1

2

2. Make his feet with four little teardrops. After you stick them onto the body, make eight tiny white balls to create his claws.

3. Use the handle of a paintbrush to make two indents for the eyes. Stick a little black ball of clay into each indent.

3

14

4. Carve in the mouth shape with a toothpick, and make two holes for the nose using the tip of a pencil. You can give him rosy cheeks by sticking on two flat pink disks.

5. Now, you just need to sculpt little triangles to make the scales on his back. Try using a different color of clay. Stick the long side of each triangle onto his back, one behind the other.

I'm so hungry!

I'm a bear

1. We're going to make a bear, starting with a slightly oval ball. Then, use a little ball (made in another color), cut it in half, and stick one half onto the body to make the bear's nose.

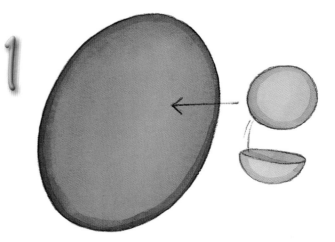

1

2. Roll out two logs, cutting off one end on each log to make them flat where they touch the ground. Make the back legs with little teardrop shapes.

2

3

3. Using a toothpick, draw a vertical line in the snout. Stick a little black ball at the top of the line for the nose.

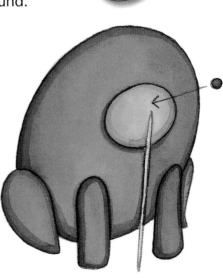

4. Make his mouth using the tip of a pencil. Then, stick on two little black balls to make the eyes.

5. Now it's time to make the ears. Just flatten two balls between your fingers, and stick them onto his head. And, don't forget his tail! Make a small worm shape and stick it on.

17

1. Start by making
a black egg shape. Then,
stick on a flattened white
ball for the penguin's
belly. Smooth it well.

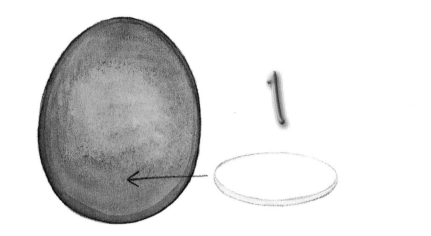

My name is pearl
the **PENGUIN**

2. Now, shape two
orange teardrop shapes
for her feet and flatten
them. Stick them onto
the bottom of the body
so she can stand up.

3. Make the beak
with a small orange
teardrop shape.
Flatten it and stick
it on in the middle,
overlapping the
white belly.

4

5. The wings are two hotdog shapes that you need to flatten. Stick just the top part of each wing onto the body. She looks cuter if the wings stick out a little bit, don't you think?

5

4. To make the eyes, flatten two white balls, then press two little black balls into the middle of each one.

Hey!!!!
Thanks for making my **feet.**
I love to **waddle!**

I'm a puppy

1. Create an oval shape for the puppy's head. Flatten two more balls, and press them onto each side of his head for the ears. Add a little black ball for his nose.

2. Use a curved piece of poster board to create the mouth. Stick on two small black balls for his eyes.

3. Make a hotdog shape for his body, and press it onto the head. Make a tongue by flattening half a red ball, and stick it onto his mouth.

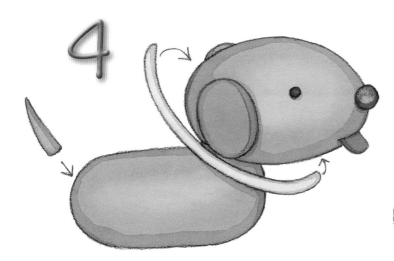

4. Roll out a long skinny piece for a collar. It will look really cute and will make the neck joint stronger. And, don't forget his tail!

5. For the legs, make a long thin hotdog shape and cut it into four equal pieces. Stick them onto the body.

my tail is up because I'm so happy!

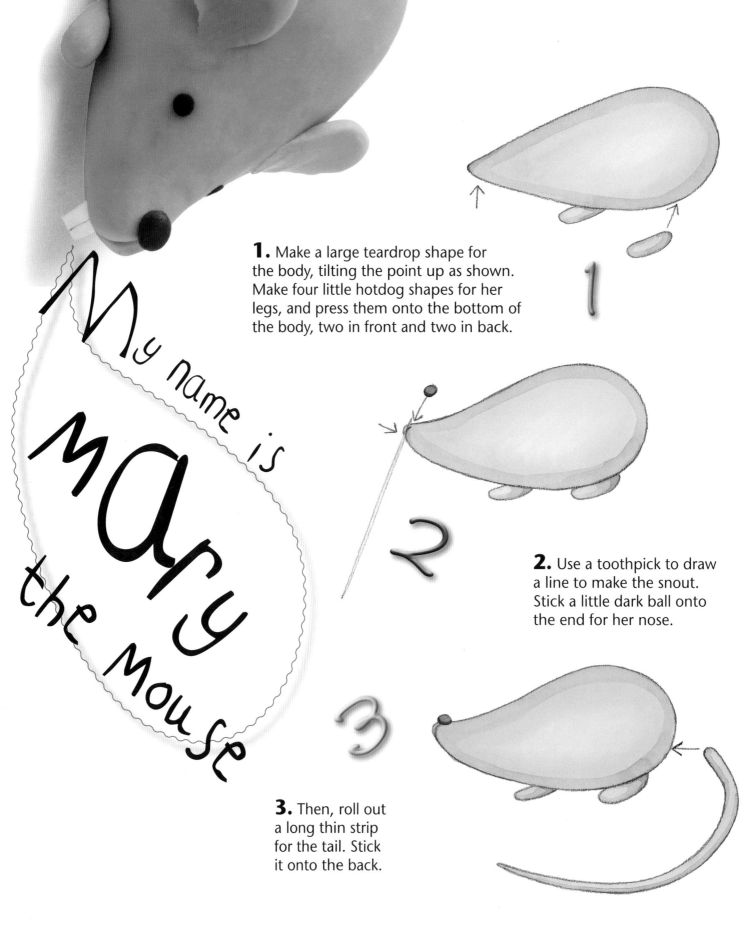

1. Make a large teardrop shape for the body, tilting the point up as shown. Make four little hotdog shapes for her legs, and press them onto the bottom of the body, two in front and two in back.

My name is **Mary** the Mouse

2. Use a toothpick to draw a line to make the snout. Stick a little dark ball onto the end for her nose.

3. Then, roll out a long thin strip for the tail. Stick it onto the back.

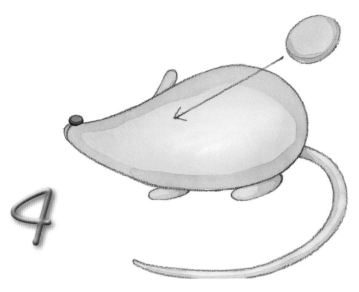

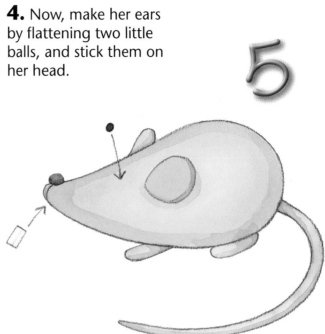

4. Now, make her ears by flattening two little balls, and stick them on her head.

5. Add two little black balls for the eyes. Finish Mary the Mouse by sticking a little white rectangle under the snout so she has teeth.

I'd like **white** teeth, please.

I'm an OWL

1. Make a large purple ball for the owl's body. Then, stick on a flattened lighter colored ball to make her belly. Smooth it out well so it blends into the body. Next, flatten two small white balls for the eyes, and stick them on.

1

2. Shape two small teardrops for her ears using purple clay. Stick them on. Then, shape two more little orange teardrops for the feet so the owl can stand.

3

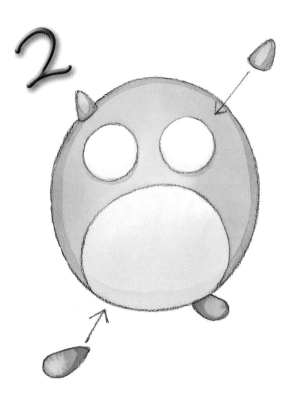

3. Another orange teardrop shape will work perfectly to make her beak. Then, press on two small black balls in the middle of the white circles for her pupils.

24

4. To make the wings, flatten two purple teardrop shapes, and stick them onto each side of the owl, with the pointy side at the top.

5. To finish, create a feather texture on her tummy using a straw at an angle.

I need great, big eyes!

1. Roll a round ball for the bunny's body. Then, make another ball with white clay and flatten it. Press it onto the body to make his belly.

2. For the legs, make four little teardrop shapes and stick them onto the body, as shown (the back legs should be a little thicker than the front ones). Add a little ball for his tail.

3. Now, make two long teardrop shapes for his ears. Flatten them before sticking them on.

My name is Bradley the Bunny

4. To make the eyes, flatten two white balls, and then stick two little black balls on top. Stick on a little pink ball for his nose, and then draw a vertical line below it with a toothpick.

5. Now you just need to make the mouth with a pencil. And don't forget to draw on his whiskers with a toothpick.

Could you make a carrot for me?

27

I'm a bee

1. 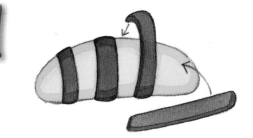 Shape a thick and short yellow log for the bee's body. Then, roll out a long black snake between your hands, flatten it slightly, and wrap strips of it around the yellow body.

2. Stick a big orange ball onto the body for the head. Make her eyes using two little yellow balls with smaller black balls on top for the pupils.

3. Make a little red ball for the nose. You can give her rosy cheeks by sticking on two flat red disks.

4. Use a curved piece of poster board to draw on the mouth. Use two pieces of plastic thread or wire to make the antennae.

5. Flatten two little white disks for the wings. Now she just needs legs, so make them with six mini black teardrop shapes.

I've eaten so much nectar!

I'm a crOcodile

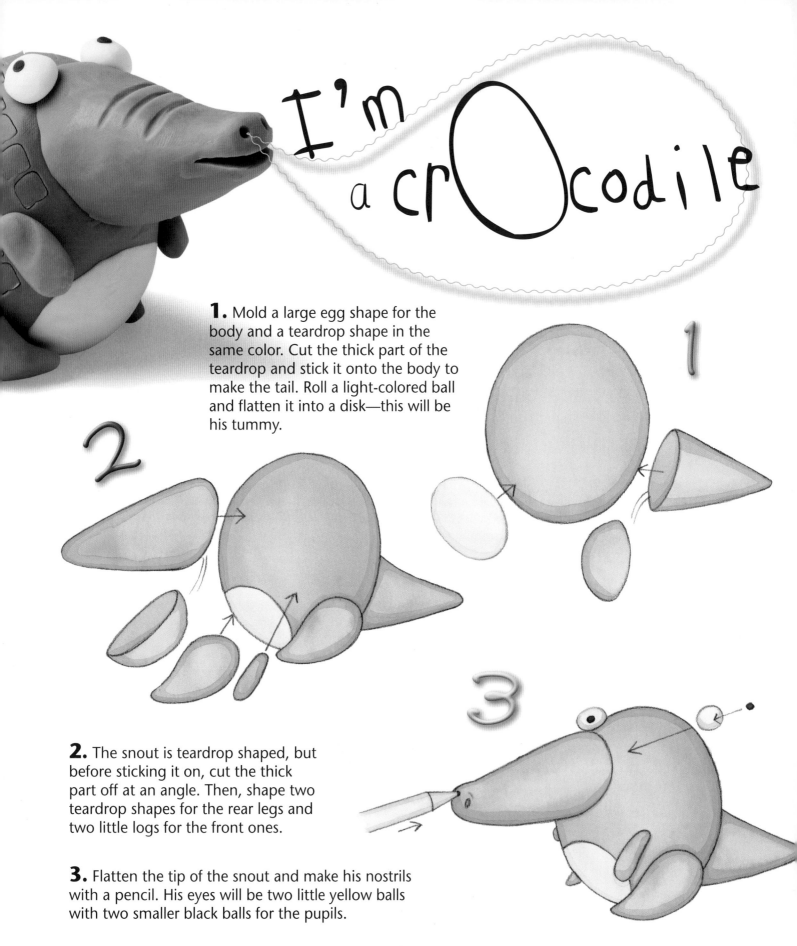

1. Mold a large egg shape for the body and a teardrop shape in the same color. Cut the thick part of the teardrop and stick it onto the body to make the tail. Roll a light-colored ball and flatten it into a disk—this will be his tummy.

2. The snout is teardrop shaped, but before sticking it on, cut the thick part off at an angle. Then, shape two teardrop shapes for the rear legs and two little logs for the front ones.

3. Flatten the tip of the snout and make his nostrils with a pencil. His eyes will be two little yellow balls with two smaller black balls for the pupils.

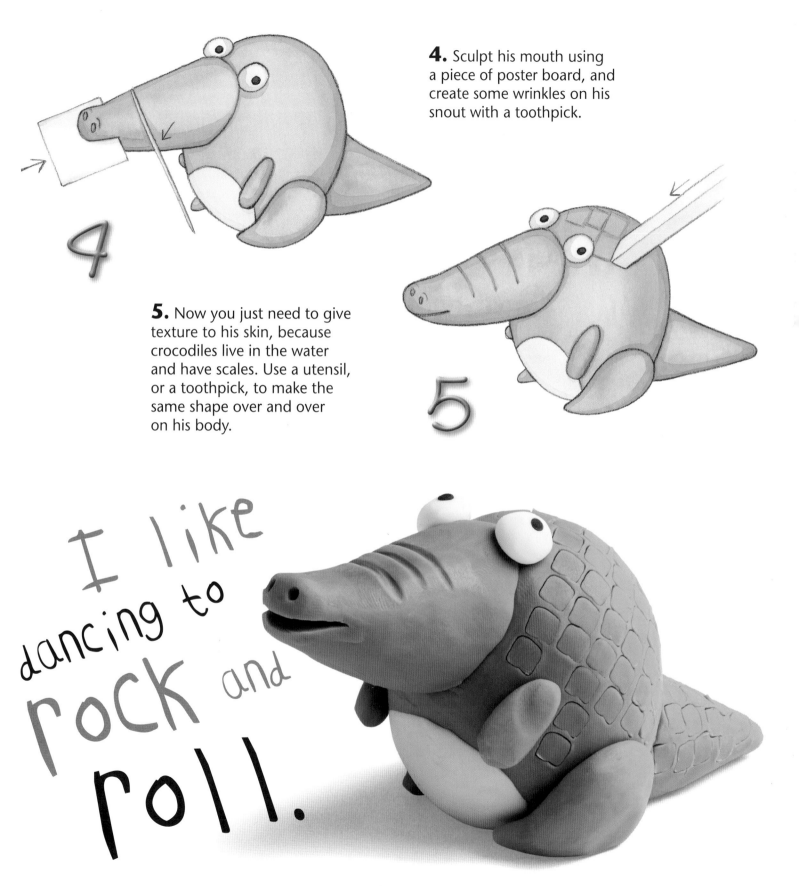

4. Sculpt his mouth using a piece of poster board, and create some wrinkles on his snout with a toothpick.

5. Now you just need to give texture to his skin, because crocodiles live in the water and have scales. Use a utensil, or a toothpick, to make the same shape over and over on his body.

I like dancing to rock and roll.

1. Mold an egg shape for the elephant's body. To make the legs, roll out a log shape between your hands, and cut it into four equal pieces. Then, stick them onto the body.

2. Roll out a thinner log for his trunk, making the end that you'll stick onto his body a bit thicker. Make a hole in the end of the trunk using the handle of a paintbrush.

My name is Eric the Elephant

3. For his big ears, shape two disks and stick them on.

32

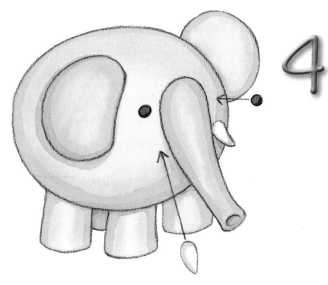

5. Elephants have little tails, so make a thin, short worm shape, and stick it on to finish.

4. Make his eyes by pressing two little black balls onto his face. And, don't forget his curved tusks, which will be two white teardrops.

make my
ears
bigger,
please.

I'm a chicken

1. To make the chicken's body, form a large egg shape, flattening the end a bit with the palm of your hand. Make it stable by pressing it lightly onto the table.

2. Now, make two flat teardrop shapes for her wings and stick them onto each side of the body. Use two smaller teardrops in another color for her feet, and her tail will be three small logs.

3. You can use a straw at an angle to make feathers on her wings and around her neck.

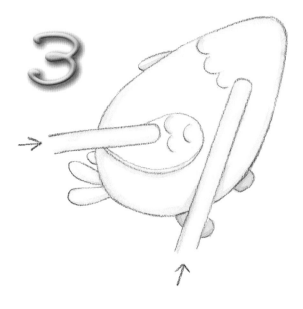

4. Make the crest with small red triangles. Make a small yellow teardrop shape for her beak.

5. To finish, make two small teardrop shapes and stick them on below her beak: This is called a wattle. Then, stick two little black balls on for the eyes.

I'm going to lay an egg!

1. Form a long teardrop shape for the seal's body, and raise the smaller end a bit.

My name is SKip the seal

2. Stick on two flattened teardrop shapes for his tail. Prepare two more teardrop shapes —slightly larger— for his flippers. Stick the narrow end of each one onto both sides of the body.

3. Flatten his two flippers so they will hold up the body, with his head raised slightly. Use two little white balls and an even smaller black one for his snout.

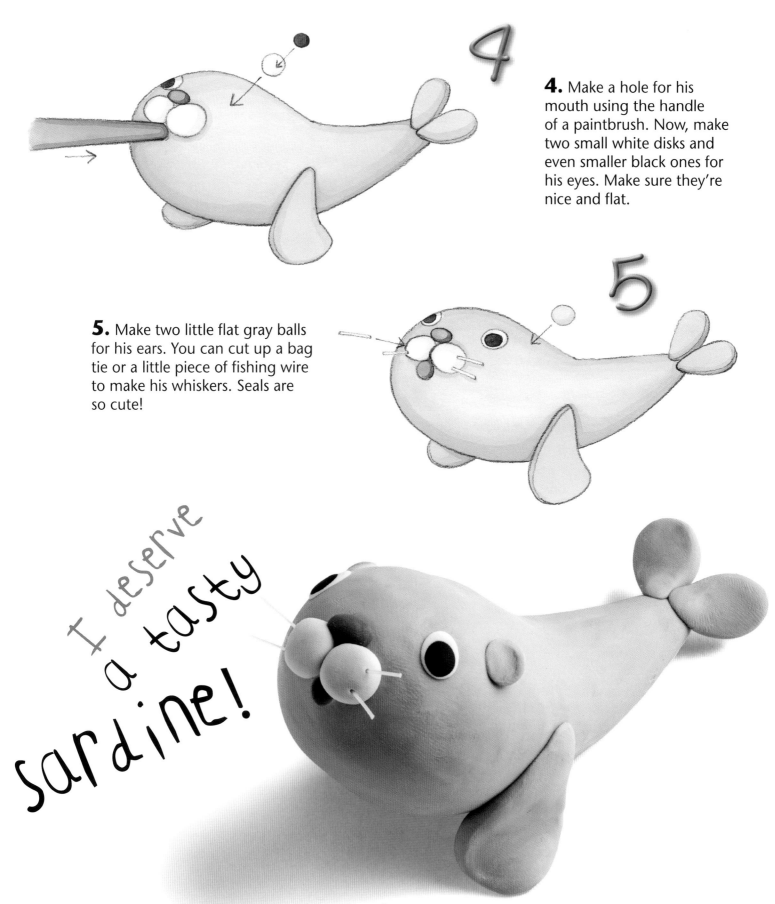

4. Make a hole for his mouth using the handle of a paintbrush. Now, make two small white disks and even smaller black ones for his eyes. Make sure they're nice and flat.

5. Make two little flat gray balls for his ears. You can cut up a bag tie or a little piece of fishing wire to make his whiskers. Seals are so cute!

I deserve a tasty sardine!

I'm a Frog

1. Make the frog's body by forming an egg shape. Make a lighter-colored disk for his tummy, and stick it on.

2. Make the back legs with two flattened balls. Then, roll out a long worm shape for his toes, and cut it into six pieces.

3. Now, make two worm shapes for his front legs. Fold them a bit so that they hold the frog up. Make two round green balls for his eyes.

1

2

3

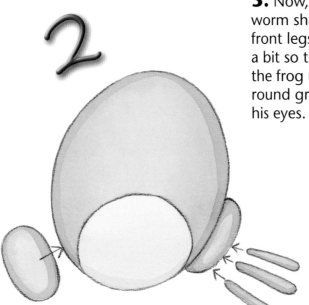

4

5

4. Now, stick two tiny black balls onto two white disks and put them onto each eye. Make two little holes for the nose using the sharp end of a pencil.

5. To finish, draw on a big smiling mouth with a toothpick.

Hug me, please!

1. Make a teardrop shape for the fox's head and a thick sausage shape for the body. Now, make two flat white teardrop shapes, which will be the chest area and for under her muzzle.

2. Make two flattened triangle shapes for the ears, and stick them onto each side of her head. Mold two little black football shapes for her eyes. Then, stick a small black ball onto the end of her snout.

3. Now it's time for the tail. Create a teardrop shape the same color as the body and another white one the same size. Cut off the end of the colored teardrop and press the end of the white teardrop onto it. Smooth the two pieces so they are joined together well, and then stick it onto the body.

My name is Fiona the FOX

40

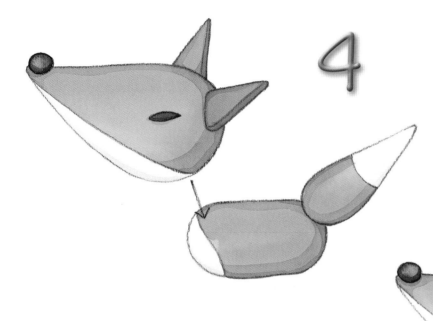

4. Join the head and body together, making the white patches on the chest and head line up. Stick toothpicks between the pieces when joining them to make your creation stronger.

5. What's left now is really easy. Roll out one long log between your hands and cut it into four equal pieces. Stick them onto the bottom of the body and… Fiona can walk now!

Look at my beautiful tail!

I'm a worm in an apple

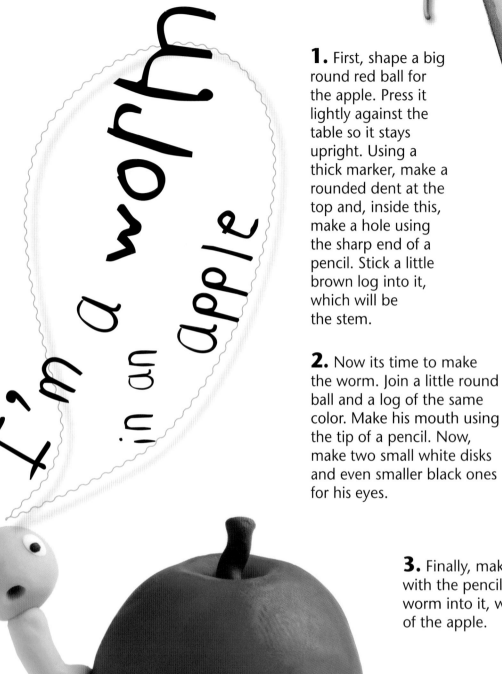

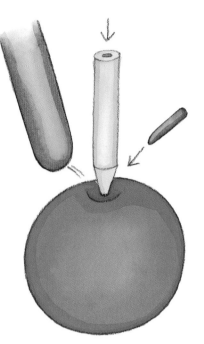

1. First, shape a big round red ball for the apple. Press it lightly against the table so it stays upright. Using a thick marker, make a rounded dent at the top and, inside this, make a hole using the sharp end of a pencil. Stick a little brown log into it, which will be the stem.

2. Now its time to make the worm. Join a little round ball and a log of the same color. Make his mouth using the tip of a pencil. Now, make two small white disks and even smaller black ones for his eyes.

3. Finally, make a hole in the apple with the pencil, and stick the hungry worm into it, where he will pop out of the apple.

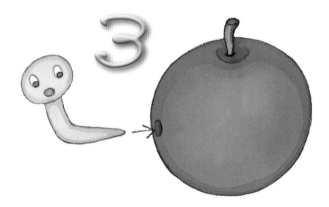

1. Shape a long log with your favorite color for the salamander's body, and make it thinner on both ends. Now, add bright-colored spots all over the body with round disks. Curve his body a little bit.

2. Stick four teardrop shapes for legs onto each side of the body, and draw on his claws with a toothpick.

3. Make the mouth with a piece of poster board and the two nostril holes with a toothpick. And, to finish, use the same color you used for his spots to make two round balls for his eyes. Add two flattened round disks (black) to create his pupils.

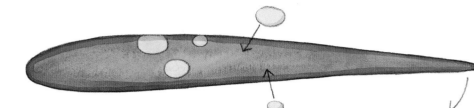

My name is Sam the salamander

43

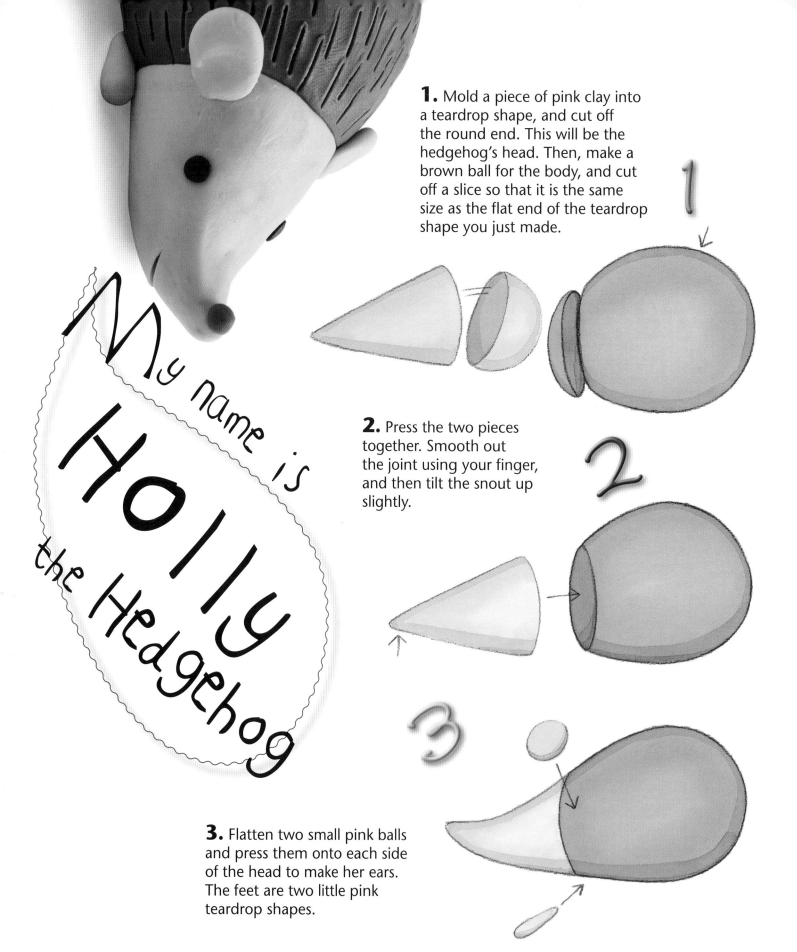

1. Mold a piece of pink clay into a teardrop shape, and cut off the round end. This will be the hedgehog's head. Then, make a brown ball for the body, and cut off a slice so that it is the same size as the flat end of the teardrop shape you just made.

1

2. Press the two pieces together. Smooth out the joint using your finger, and then tilt the snout up slightly.

2

3. Flatten two small pink balls and press them onto each side of the head to make her ears. The feet are two little pink teardrop shapes.

3

My name is Holly the Hedgehog

44

4. Press two tiny black balls for eyes onto the snout and a brown ball onto the end for her nose.

5. To finish, use a piece of poster board to create her mouth. You can make her quills by marking short lines onto her body with a toothpick.

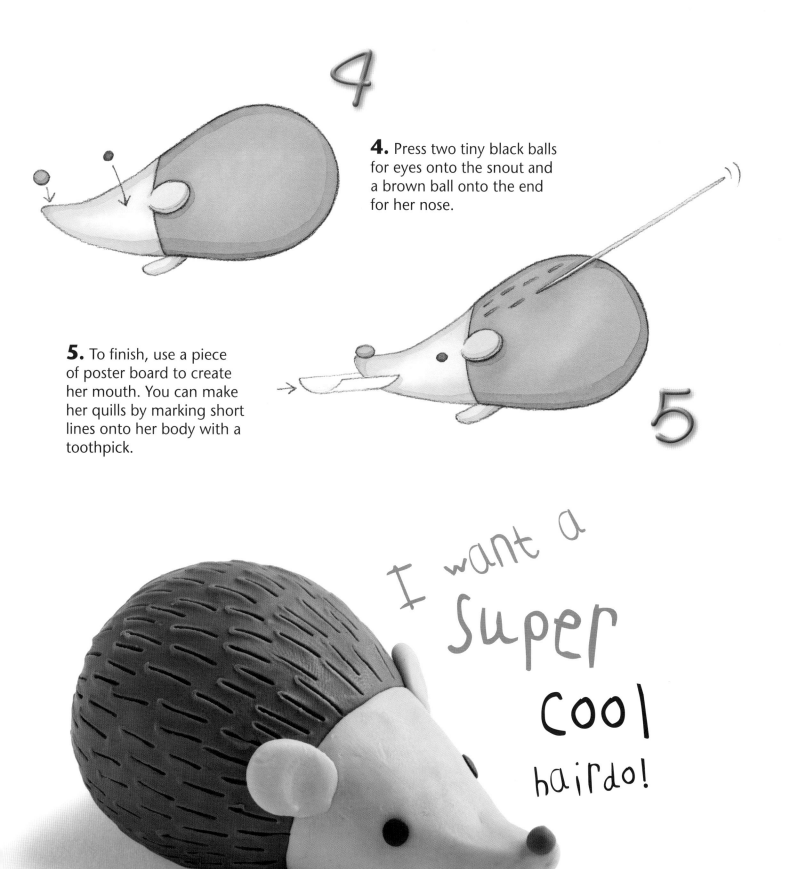

I want a super cool hairdo!

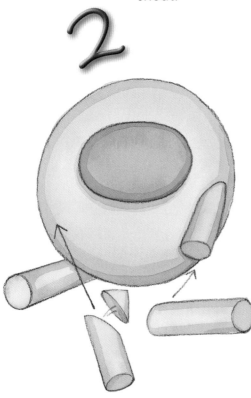

I'm a hippo

1. Shape a round ball for the hippo's body. Make a smaller oval ball in another color. Cut it in half and stick one of the halves onto the big ball to make the snout.

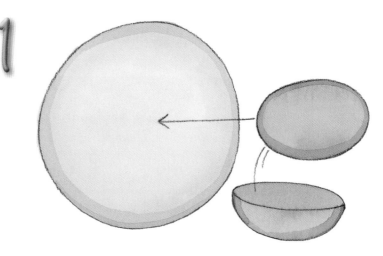

2. Make a log and cut it in half for the back legs. Stick them onto the hippo, a little open, so he will stay sitting up. Use a smaller log and cut it in half for the two front legs. Cut them at an angle so they fit better.

3. Stick two little balls of the same color as the snout for his nose, making holes with a pencil. Use a piece of poster board to carve the shape of his mouth.

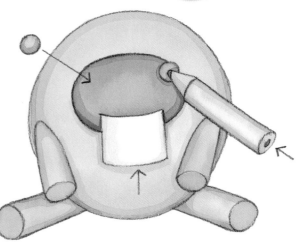

4. Use the same color to make two little balls for his ears. Flatten them a little, and make a dent in the middle before sticking them onto the head. His eyes will be two more little balls with two little black balls for pupils.

5. For his tail, just stick on a thin log. And, to finish, you can add nails with little white balls.

I like to **soak** in the water.

47

1. Start by making a ball for the koala's body. Cut off a piece at the top so the head will fit better. Then, make a white flat disk and press it into the body for her belly.

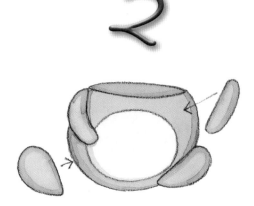

2. Next, shape two little logs for the front legs and two larger logs for the back ones.

My name is Kelly the **koala**

 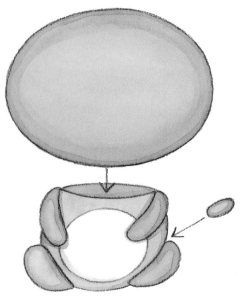

3. Shape a bigger oval ball for her head and press it into the body. Add a little gray hotdog shape for her tail.

48

4

4. To make her nose, cut a thick dark log in half and stick it onto the middle of her face. Give her big ears using two flattened disks.

5

5. To finish, stick two little black balls on for the eyes. Now you just need to make her smile. Use a toothpick to draw it on.

I want to hug you!

1. For the turtle's shell, make a ball and cut it in half. Then, make different-sized disks in a darker tone, and stick them onto the shell.

2. Roll out a long thin log in the same color as the shell and wrap it around the bottom. Make sure you press it in nice and tight all the way around so it stays together.

3. Make six teardrop shapes using another color: four the same size for her legs, a big one for her head, and a final smaller one for her tail. Press them all onto the edge of the shell, except for the tail, which will go on the wide part of the shell.

I'm a turtle

4. Create the mouth using a piece of poster board.

5. Finish your turtle with two tiny black balls to give her eyes.

Please, **wait** for me!

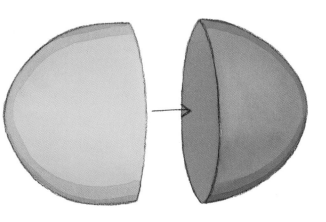

1. Make two balls using different colors. Cut them both in half and join one half of each color. Smooth the two halves together well. This will be the head and body.

2. To make her tail, mold a teardrop shape the same color as the body and flatten it. Cut off the narrow end and draw on some lines with a toothpick. Stick it onto the body.

My name is Fran the fish

3. Make a ball shape for the mouth, and then make a hole in the middle using the handle of a paintbrush. Now, make two small white balls and even smaller black ones for her eyes.

1

2

3

4. Holding a straw at an angle, press it into the body to make her scales.

5. And what would a fish be without gills? Stick two flattened teardrop shapes onto each side of the body. You can draw lines to define the scales, and then make some more for the top of her body. Use your imagination!

Nothing scares me.

I'm a CoW

1. We're going to make a round cow sitting down, so we'll start with a ball for the body. Then, shape another smaller ball in another color and cut it in half: one half will be her snout and the other her udder. Stick them onto the body, as shown.

2. Stick two little balls of the same color onto her udder. Make two holes in her snout with a pencil, and give her a nice big smile using a piece of poster board.

3. For the legs, make a long thin hotdog shape and cut it into four equal pieces. It's better to cut the front legs at an angle so they fit well. Spread the back legs out on both sides of her body so she can sit down.

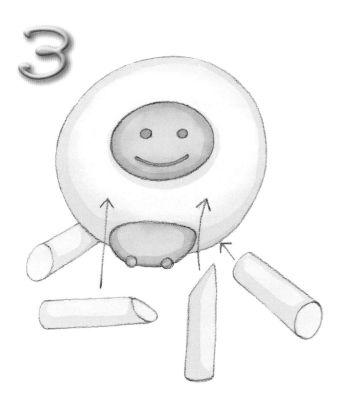

4

5

4. Draw a line onto the back legs with a toothpick to make the hooves. Stick two teardrop shapes onto the head for her ears. The eyes will be two little black balls above the snout.

5. Now make two little white teardrops for the horns. And her spots? You know how to do it! Use flattened circles and stick them all over the body.

I say "moo!"

1

1. Making a snake is so easy. Roll out a long snake shape and decorate it with different-sized disks in a different color.

2

2. Coil him up. Make the head with a teardrop shape and stick it onto the body.

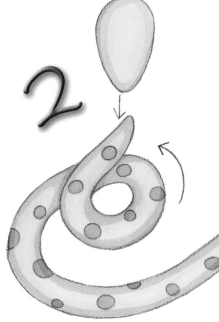

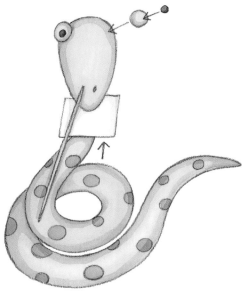

3

3. The eyes will be two little balls the same color as the body, with two black pupils on top. Use a toothpick to make his nostrils, and use poster board to create the mouth.

My name is Sid the snake

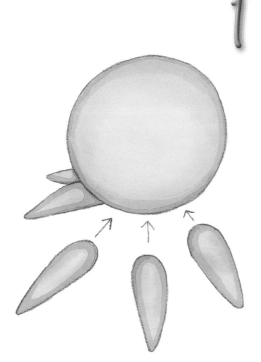

1. Make a ball for the body and eight long teardrop shapes in the same color. Arrange the teardrop shapes —her tentacles—all around the body. Join them by pressing them together.

2. Then, make three little balls. Stick one on for her mouth, making a hole in the middle with the handle of a paintbrush. The other two smaller ones will be the eyes.

3. Stick two little black balls on for the pupils. To finish, make lots of different-sized small balls in another color, and stick them all over her body.

I'm an octopus

I'm a Kitten

1. If you want to create a Siamese kitten, mix white with a bit of yellow, a touch of brown, and a little blue. Make two balls in this color, one larger than the other, and join them together. Use the larger ball for the head and the smaller one for the body.

2. Using dark brown clay, make two little balls for her snout. Stick a tiny black ball in the middle for her little nose.

3. Draw a vertical line under the snout and then a mouth, using a toothpick. Hold a straw at an angle to create her closed eyelids. Shhh, she's sleeping…

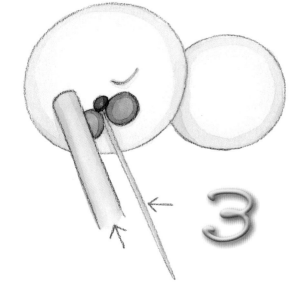

4. For the ears, make two flattened teardrop shapes in dark brown. You can use fishing wire to make her whiskers.

5. For the front paws, make two logs the same color as the body and stick them on, as shown. To finish, mold a log using dark brown clay for her tail, and stick it on.

It is so comfy here...

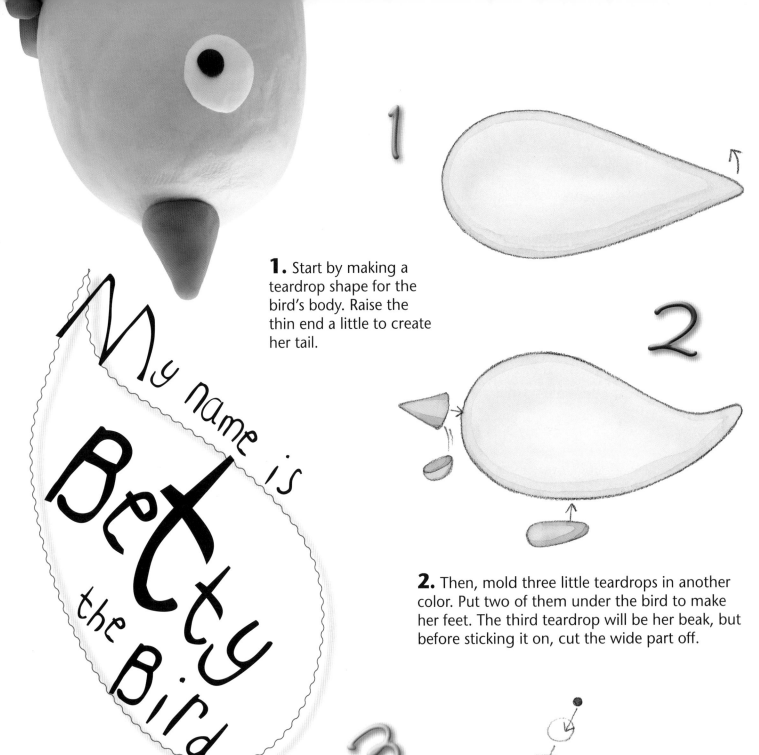

My name is Betty the Bird

1. Start by making a teardrop shape for the bird's body. Raise the thin end a little to create her tail.

2. Then, mold three little teardrops in another color. Put two of them under the bird to make her feet. The third teardrop will be her beak, but before sticking it on, cut the wide part off.

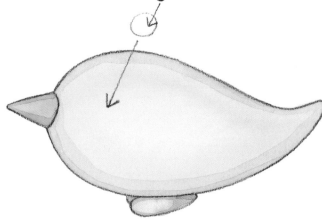

3. Stick a white disk onto each side of her head with a little black ball inside each one. Now she can see!

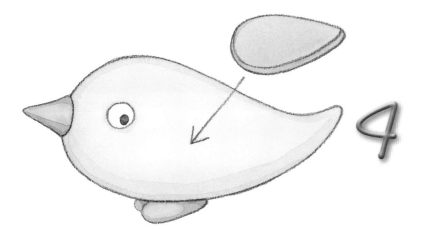

4. The wings are two flat teardrop shapes, one on each side. You could use a darker tone than the body or even a totally different color.

5. To finish, make feathers on her wings by holding a straw at an angle, and press lightly into the clay. Now, let's see if she'll sing you a song!

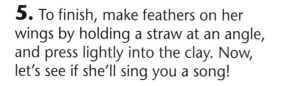

I am blue like the sky.

I'm a Chick

1. Make an oval ball for the chick's body, and two little teardrops in another color for his feet. Place them under the body and press down slightly so that he is stable.

1

2. To make the beak, mold a little teardrop shape the same color as the feet and press it on using your finger.

2

3

3. Stick two little white disks on for the eyes.

4. Don't forget to add two little black balls in the middle of the white disks to make the pupils.

5. Two slightly-flattened log shapes are the final step to make your little chick's wings.

Did you model a mom for me?

1. Start by molding two teardrops with different colors. One will be the squirrel's body and the other his big tail. Bend the thin ends a little.

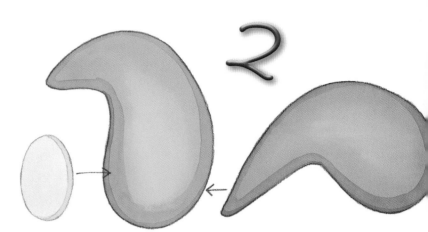

2. To make his belly, pick a light color. Make a disk and stick it in place. Now, join the tail and body by pressing them together. You can rub the joint underneath to make it more secure.

My name is Simon the Squirrel

3. Make his legs with four teardrop shapes the same color as his body. The front legs should be a little smaller. Join them to the body by pressing them on at the wider end.

4. Make two teardrop shapes for his ears. Then, make a tiny little ball the same color as the tail for his nose.

5. To finish, add two little black balls for the eyes. Then, give him some long teeth with a small piece of poster board—without them he can't eat acorns!

I lost my acorn!

65

I'm a ladybug

1. Start by shaping a red ball for the ladybug's body, and then flatten it slightly with the palm of your hand. Then, make a pink disk and press it over one end of the body to make her face.

2. Draw a line with a toothpick to make her wings. Stick lots of little black balls all over the body to make her spots.

3. To make the eyes, stick two little black balls onto two white disks. Give her a big smile by pressing a curved piece of poster board, as shown.

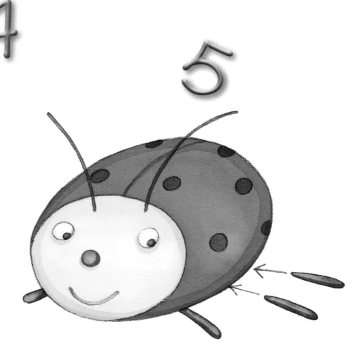

4. Stick a little red ball onto her face to make the nose. For the antennae, you could use two pieces of black nylon thread.

5. To make the legs, stick three thin log shapes onto each side of her body. That was easy, wasn't it?

Do you like my polka-dots?

1

My name is Ray the Reindeer

1. Make two oval balls for the reindeer's head and body, and rub them together where they join underneath. If you like this color, you can make it by adding a little brown, yellow, and black to white clay.

2

2. Roll out a thin snake shape the same color between your hands, and cut it into four equal parts to make his legs. Put the legs under the body, like you see in the drawing. Create his hooves by adding a dark cone shape to the end of each leg.

3

3. Draw a line in the middle of each hoof with a toothpick. Make his tail with a little teardrop shape the same color as the body.

68

4. Holding a straw at an angle, press into the face to make his eyelids (quietly, we don't want to wake him up!). Add a red ball to make his nose.

5. The ears are two teardrop shapes stuck onto the head. Now you just need to find a couple of twigs to make his antlers.

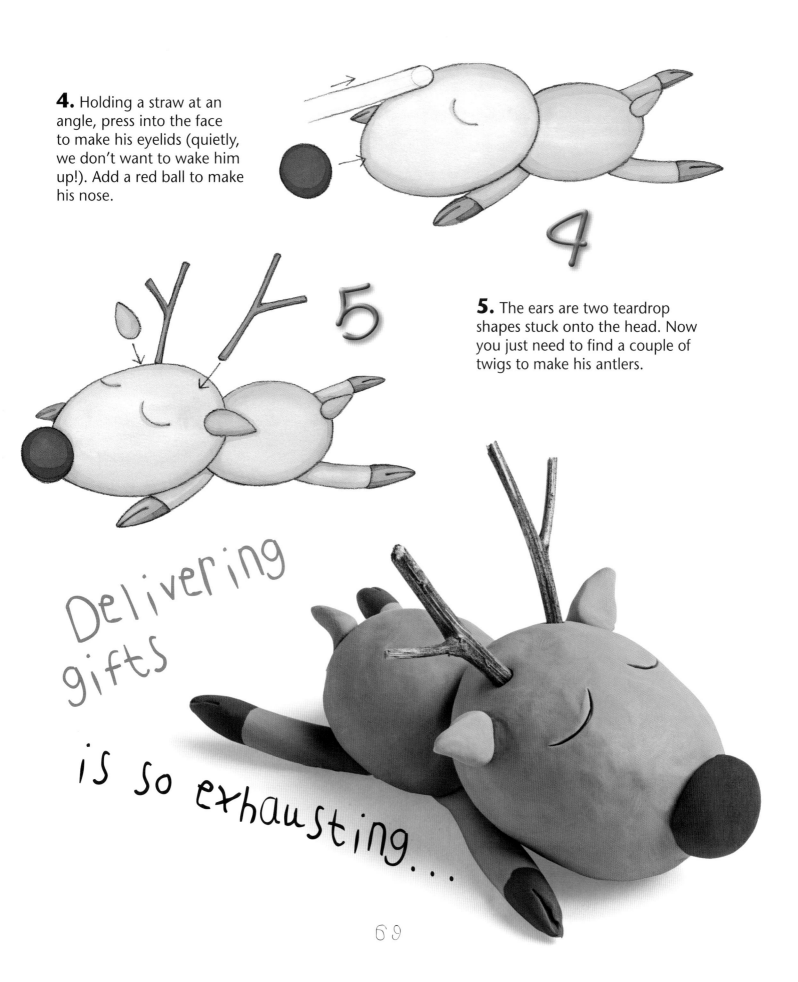

Delivering gifts

is so exhausting...

I'm a toucan

1. Shape a black ball for the toucan's body. Then, press a white disk onto it to make the belly.

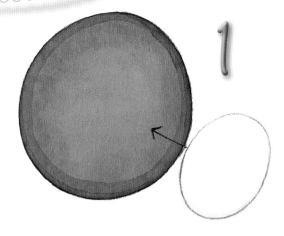

2. A black flat teardrop shape will be the tail. Then, add two flat balls for the feet—these will give your tropical bird good balance.

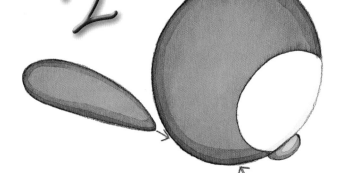

3. Now it's time to make his famous orange beak. Make a teardrop shape and cut off the wide part before sticking it onto the head. Finish the tail by drawing a line down the middle with a toothpick.

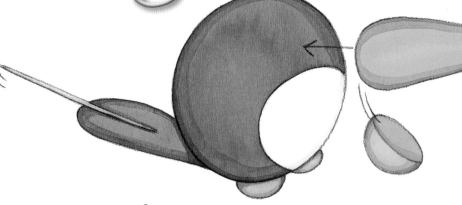

70

4. Curve the end of the beak down a little, as shown. To make the eyes, stick on two blue disks with little black balls in the middle.

5. Finish the toucan by adding a wing to each side of his body. He looks real, doesn't he?

I'm proud

of my

beak!

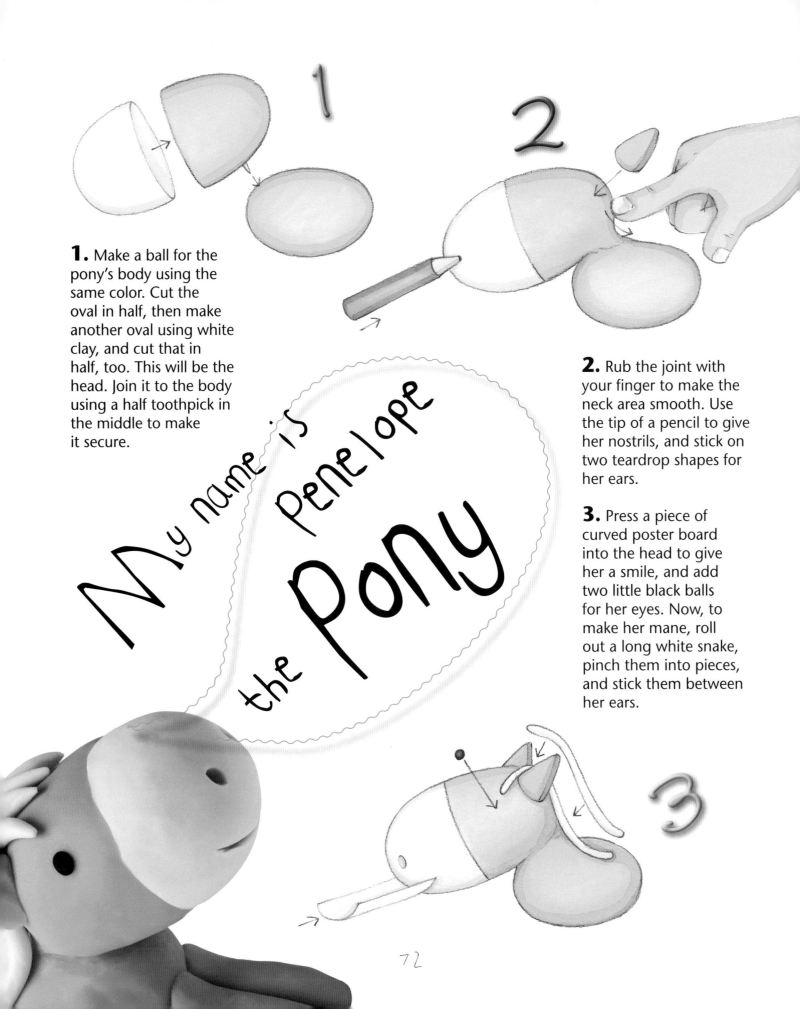

1. Make a ball for the pony's body using the same color. Cut the oval in half, then make another oval using white clay, and cut that in half, too. This will be the head. Join it to the body using a half toothpick in the middle to make it secure.

2. Rub the joint with your finger to make the neck area smooth. Use the tip of a pencil to give her nostrils, and stick on two teardrop shapes for her ears.

3. Press a piece of curved poster board into the head to give her a smile, and add two little black balls for her eyes. Now, to make her mane, roll out a long white snake, pinch them into pieces, and stick them between her ears.

My name is Penelope the Pony

4. For the legs, make a long hotdog shape and cut it into four equal pieces. Stick two on the front and two on the back. If you open them up, it will look like she's jumping.

5. To make sure she's stable, cut a bit off the bottom of the legs at an angle, so they line up with the table. Add a tail by sticking on a couple of white snakes. And, she's ready to go!

Do you want to brush my mane?

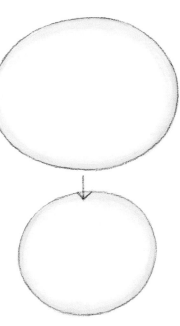

I'm a panda

1. Mold two white balls, one smaller than the other. Join them together firmly. The little one will be the panda's body, and the other will be his head.

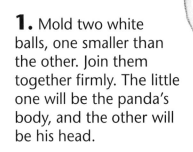

2. Roll out a black log and wrap it around his neck from behind, so that the ends create the arms. Smooth it in the back with your finger so everything is joined together well. For the legs, put two black teardrop shapes under the body.

3. Make his snout from half of a white ball. For his ears, shape two disks and stick them onto the top of his head.

4. Finish his snout by drawing a vertical line with a toothpick. He also needs a nose, which you can make with another little black ball.

4

5

5. Now, make his eyes with two flat oval disks. Stick them onto the face, then add two little white balls in the middle. Finish with two more tiny black balls.

I eat bamboo all day long!

My name is Shelly the Sheep

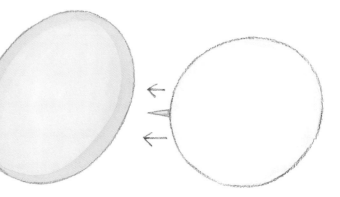

1. Make a ball for the sheep's body and a slightly larger oval shape for her head. Join them together using half a toothpick so it stays secure.

2. Should we make her wool now? Stick lots of little balls all over her body, except for underneath. Also, press little balls onto her head. Make a long teardrop shape and stick it on the back for her tail.

3. The ears will be two more teardrop shapes the same color as the wool. To make her eyes really pop, stick on two balls, the same color as the head. Then, add two little white balls. Finally, add two tiny black balls for the pupils.

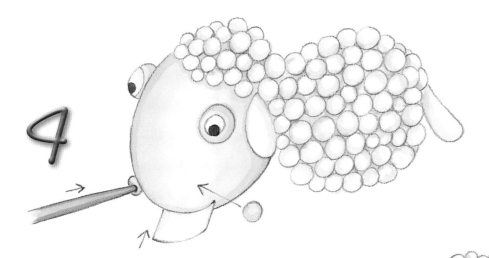

4. For the nose, stick on two little balls and make a hole in the end of each with the handle of a paintbrush. Press a little piece of poster board into her face to create her mouth.

5. She's only missing legs now! Make them by shaping four logs the same color as the head. Make her legs short because she is heavy and we don't want her to fall, right?

Have you seen the wolf?

I'm a hamster

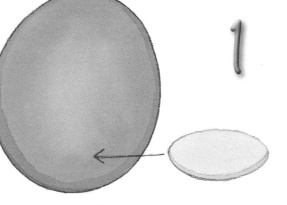

1. Start by making an oval ball for the hamster's body. Give him a belly by sticking on a light-colored disk. Smooth it well over the body.

2. Now, make the front legs by sticking two little teardrops onto the sides. For the back legs, make two little balls and smoosh the body down onto them. You can make the tail with a little log shape.

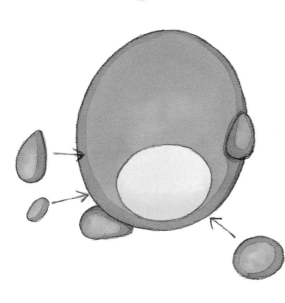

3. To make the ears, make two small flattened balls the same color as the body. Then, using the same color as the belly, stick two more little balls inside. Cut off one side of each circle so the ears fit onto the head better. A half ball, the same color as the belly, will be the snout.

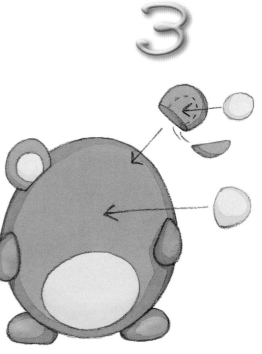

4. Draw a vertical line on the snout with a toothpick. Then, stick a little black ball in the middle for the nose. Add two more little black balls for the eyes.

5. To finish, use a small rectangular piece of poster board to make the teeth. Then, use little pieces of nylon wire or thread for the whiskers.

Look at my cute ears...

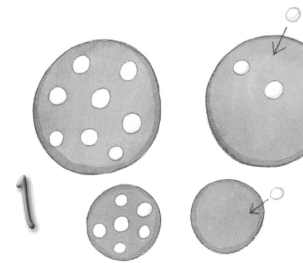

1. Start by making the butterfly's wings with four balls, two bigger than the others. Flatten them and decorate them with lots of little balls in a different color. If you have a roller, use it so her wings are nice and even.

My name is Brenda the **Butterfly**

2. Put the little wings behind the big ones, as shown. Then, stick a log shape that's narrow at the ends onto the wings for her body. Rub them in well on the back to join them securely.

3. Holding a straw at an angle, press it into the body to make her mouth.

4. Make two little balls for the eyes and two tiny black balls for her pupils. You can make the nose with a short piece of plastic, like a bag tie.

5. For her antennae, use thick nylon thread. Finish by sticking on six tiny hotdog shapes for her legs.

I'm Ready to **fly!**

I'm a monkey

1. After making a big ball for the monkey's head, stick on a flat disk in a light color for his face. Then, stick on two flat disks on each side of the head. Now he has ears!

2. Stick two little black balls on for the eyes. Use a toothpick to draw a line to make the snout.

3. Use the tip of a pencil to make a hole for his mouth, then add a little ball for his nose.

4. Mold a thick barrel shape for his body. Join it to the head, and flatten it slightly onto the table so he sits up.

5. Now, roll out a long thin snake. Cut it into several pieces: two pieces for the arms, two longer pieces for the legs—bending them at his knees—and the longest piece for his tail.

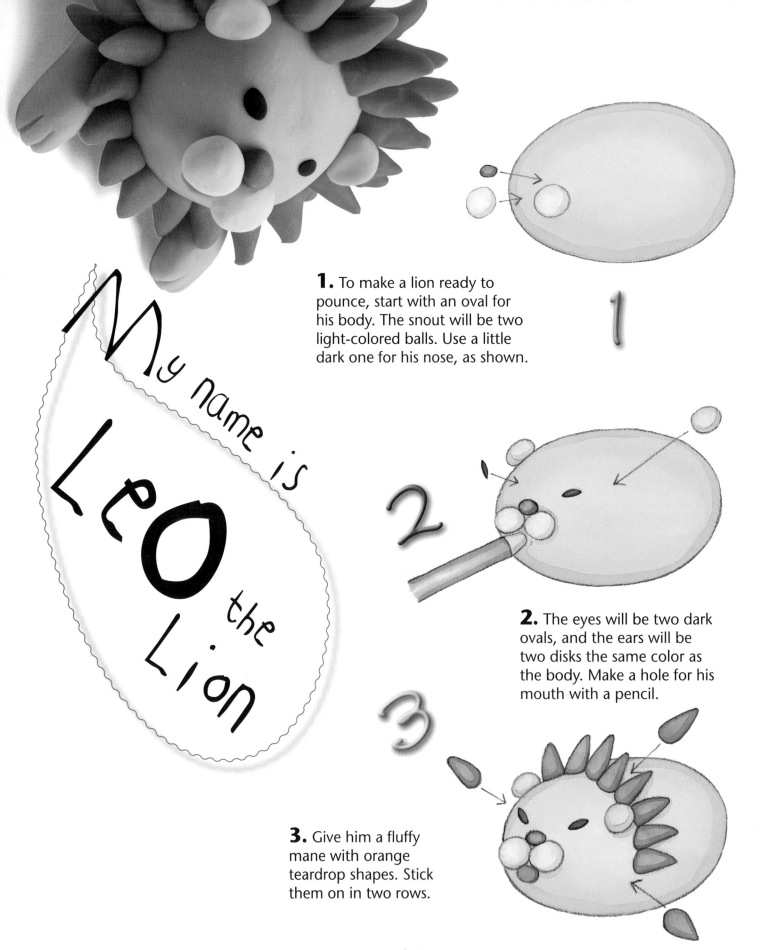

My name is LeO the Lion

1. To make a lion ready to pounce, start with an oval for his body. The snout will be two light-colored balls. Use a little dark one for his nose, as shown.

2. The eyes will be two dark ovals, and the ears will be two disks the same color as the body. Make a hole for his mouth with a pencil.

3. Give him a fluffy mane with orange teardrop shapes. Stick them on in two rows.

4. Now it's time to make his legs. Mold two logs for the front and two teardrops for the back.

5. Draw on sharp claws on his front paws using a toothpick. To make his tail, roll out a log the same color as the body and stick on an orange teardrop shape at the tip.

It's a fun day in the jungle!

I'm a raccoon

1. Roll a big barrel shape for the raccoon's body and cut off the ends so they're flat. Make a flat white oval and stick it onto the body for his tummy. The head will be an oval shape. Stick two black disk shapes on the head to create his eye mask.

2. Join the head and body together. Now, make two small white disks and even smaller black ones for his eyes.

3. Make his front legs with two little logs the same color as his body. The back legs will be two black teardrop shapes.

4. Use a piece of poster board to carve the shape of his mouth. For the ears, stick two little black triangles into two slightly larger triangles the same color as the body. Don't forget his nose! Stick on a small black ball.

5. Now he just needs a tail. Roll out a white teardrop shape and wrap flattened black stripes around it. Join them together by rolling it on the table, and then stick it onto the body.

I'm ready to **find** food!

1

2

1. Start by making a ball for the deer's body. Then, make a small flat light-colored disk for her belly and join it to the body. Make two logs for her back legs so she sits up. Draw on two lines with a toothpick for the hooves.

My name is Daphne the Deer

2. Make two longer thinner logs for her front legs. Then, make a big egg shape for her head, and stick it onto the body.

3

3. Draw on a vertical line for the snout using a toothpick, and use a straw to make the mouth. For her ears, make two triangle shapes the same color as the body.

4. Give her a nose and eyes with black balls. Flatten the balls for the eyes a little bit.

5. Stick on a little teardrop shape for the tail. Now, make several little balls in the same color you used for the belly, flattening them onto the body to give her spots. Find little twigs for the antlers, and stick them on.

My antlers are unique!

1. Make a big teardrop shape for the wolf's body. Tilt it up a bit and add a flat light-colored disk for the belly. Round the end of the teardrop.

I'm a wolf

2. To help him sit, add two fat little teardrops under his body and two longer thinner ones in front (bend the paws a bit so he'll sit up better).

3. Make his howling mouth using the end of a marker.

4. Stick on two flattened teardrop shapes for his ears. Make his tail with a log that is pointy on both ends.

5. Add two little black half-moons and a ball, so he can see and smell.

Today there is a full **moon!**

I'm a kanga roo

1. Shape the kangaroo's body into a long teardrop shape, and bend it at the narrow end to make her head. Roll out a log and cut it straight across at the thick end before sticking it onto the body. Then, make another flat half-moon shape and stick it onto the body. That's her pouch.

2. The arms are two little flat logs. To make the legs, join a flattened ball and a teardrop together for each one.

3. Create the mouth with poster board, and make two flat triangles for her ears.

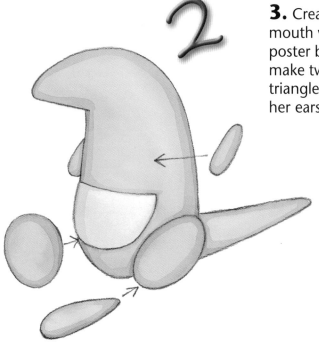

4. Now you need three little black balls: two flattened ones for her eyes and a round one for the nose.

5. Mama kangaroo is all done now. Do you want to make her a baby? Make little teardrop shapes for the head and ears and stick on tiny black balls for the baby's nose and eyes.

My sweet baby is hungry.

93

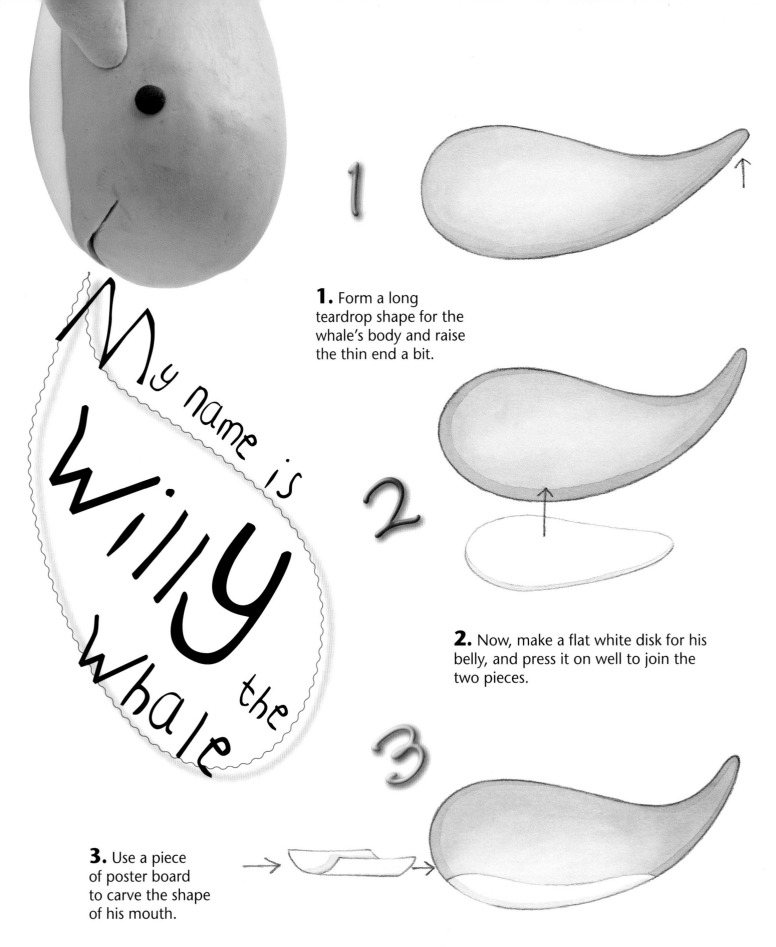

My name is Willy the whale

1. Form a long teardrop shape for the whale's body and raise the thin end a bit.

2. Now, make a flat white disk for his belly, and press it on well to join the two pieces.

3. Use a piece of poster board to carve the shape of his mouth.

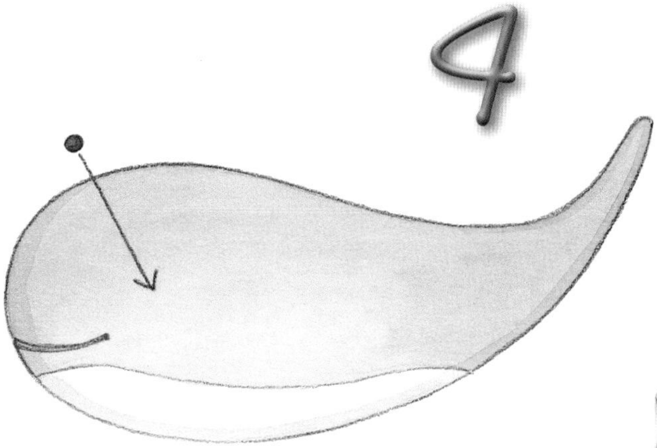

4. Press two little black balls on for his eyes.

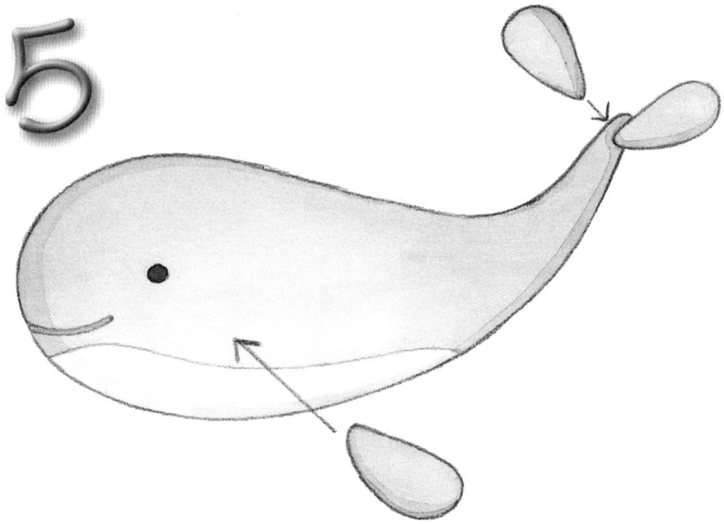

5. You can make the fins with two flattened teardrop shapes. Stick the narrow end onto each side and now do the same for the tail.

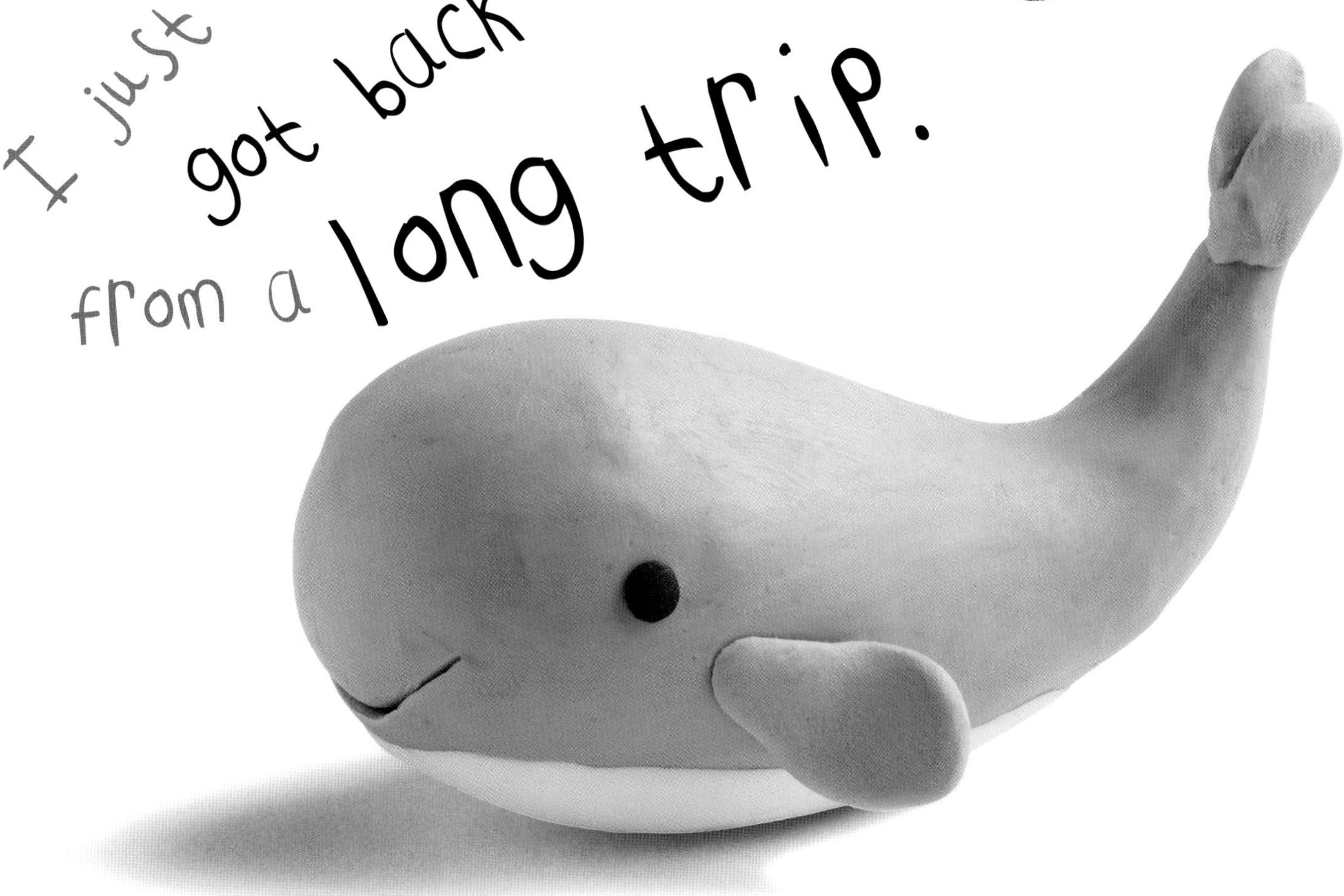
I just got back from a long trip.

First edition for North America published
in 2016 by B.E.S. Publishing Co.

© Gemser Publications, S.L. 2016
El Castell, 38 08329 Teiá (Barcelona, Spain)
www.mercedesros.com

Idea: Georgina Segarra
Text, illustrations, and figure modeling: Bernadette Cuxart
Design and layout: Estudi Guasch, S.L.
Photography: Pep Herrero

All inquiries should be addressed to:
Peterson's Publishing, LLC
4380 S. Syracuse Street, Suite 200
Denver, CO 80237-2624
www.petersonsbooks.com

ISBN: 978-1-4380-0908-7

Library of Congress Control No.:
2016931355

Date of Manufacture: December 2020
Manufactured by: L. Rex Printing
Company Limited, Dongguan City,
Guangdong, China

Printed in China

9 8 7 6 5